Blue Dynamite

a narrative

John Millett

POETRY AUSTRALIA

Number 106, 1986

Editor: Grace Perry, A.M.

Published by SOUTH HEAD PRESS

with the assistance of the Literature Board of the Australia Council, the Federal Governments' Arts Funding Advisory Body, The New South Wales Government Office of the Minister for The Arts and The Peter Stuyvesant Cultural Foundation

The big 'Bluebirds' are rolling in; gigantic waves that sweep in from the horizon on extraordinary occasions.

– Duke Kahanamoku.

First published in 1986 by
SOUTH HEAD PRESS
The Market Place, Berrima, NSW 2577

National Library of Australia
card number and ISBN 0 909 185 28 X
Wholly set up and printed in Australia by Hogbin, Poole (Printers Pty. Ltd.
99 Marriott Street, Redfern, NSW 2016

CHAPTER 1

BODHISATTVA

Hot Dogger Sunday

A young hotty
plays to the telephoto barrage
on the cliff
pushes out for a mid-day
low tide barrel session

does aerials under the lip-snap
backward verticals, cut-backs
upsidedown re-entries
into a cover up
carves tracks
bounces off the light
backsliding
slashing in a space age lifestyle

a prophet loose in body and mind
in touch with the sea
cranks a bottom turn
up the ledge to throw himself
at the sky arms outstretched
totally hitting it
with a flying off-the-lip

then out-back
to cruise for waves
along Two Mile Reef
feel push and power in the slush
sea-spin
listen to winds hollowing
the oldest latitudes in the world
taste dead sailors
slice home on late afternoon glass
switched into circuits of the sun

Sydney Grommets

Early morning boardriders
wax hulls
that will letter young waves
with signwriting from their own bodies
inscribe theorems on the morning skyline
craft italics on The Tasman
as they lean and swerve and flash
along triangles where every force is cancelled

The beach on the city's edge
divides a sea primitive as Bedouins
from tower blocks

These boardriders need not edit
the tides' transcript
on white sand
They know the encyclopaedia east winds write
cool pleats of early cirrus
angles where their own italics are wiped out
dog-eared streets
on which they turn their backs
for wet suits

Precisely at nine o'clock
they sign the high water mark
become architects   planners
property developers   barristers
planing the glass surface of commerce
each with the sea's religion
in his blood

Managing Director

Word processors begin work exactly at 9
filling paper spaces of the world
with laser print-outs
no one could read in a lifetime
spaced-out jargon of commerce
the LSD of executives
who blow as soon as they see a spread-sheet

Mr Wang is always user-friendly
never out of line
Softly his software digests feed-in
taste and touch sensitive to every integer

The office floor is serious about dirt
Office walls always smile
Windows polish early sunlight on the harbour
Chairs take the micky out of buttocks
then kiss them on the cheeks
She's apples. No hard feelings mate

Roger sits at his desk with an amber phosphor monitor
and Mr Wang sits quietly on-line
megabytes of RAM under his belt
retrieves whatever stick is thrown for him
chases through kilobytes
expanded to the nth power by modems
wags his tail at binary arithmetic
obedient as a well-trained spaniel
protective as a doberman

Whatever command is given
Mr Wang in his shy enamel suit
treats as a war game
He is the mascot of storm troopers
who do not flinch
at falling dollar signs
Mr Wang prints in clean pixels
to multidirectional centronics
in parallel port

The MD pats his alpha-numeric function
and Mr Wang wags a tail
filled with the wisdom of the Orient

Chinese Doll on the Office Credenza

That figure in the glass case
Silk garments
embroidered by someone
with a flair to make stitches
into peacock tails
someone with skills
longer than fingernails
and the trick of knowing
when to stop curl and camber of curves
that jump from cloth
pat lazy days in her lap
hold at arms length
the lunge and stretch of thread
appraise what's done
rhythms old as Manchuria

Some woman who lives anywhere
strong fingers
level eyes
full of children
needing no calendar
to read scrawls of frost
at her door

Someone not threatened by loss
who enters the slow presence of ships
weighing anchor
waves goodbye to a sailor
goes on home
a place close by
where the sun is rich

all her politics in one needle
history in colored threads

Meteoric House

On the 40th Floor of Meteoric House
the telephone winks its electronic eye
The switch girl in a voice soft as a Chinese carpet

The Minister for Contrivances
returning your call

Connect me

the MD taps his pencil

John I'd like to speak with you
again about Greenville over lunch

OK to meet you at the club Thursday?

Right – then it's 1 o'clock

We'd need 2 hours I'd say

Roger noted the appointment – January 12
put the handpiece into its blue cradle
where it slept peacefully for 10 minutes
asked for the Sydney Outline Map
black instant coffee

No more calls this morning

I'm working on a scheme
to take over Greenville

where it sleeps plaited into the raw half-light of elms
planted in the darkness of eighteen fifty three
old houses shawled like grandmothers
churches where Parish Registers hide
records of deaths entered carelessly
by O'Briens and Ahearns whose rusty voices led choirs
at marriages within prohibited degrees
of consanguinity and affinity
which may explain IQs below the poverty line
recessive genes of Greens
who could talk only to honeyeaters at back doors
tell time by sunrise and sunset

the month by what berry was ripe for eating
winter by the thickness of fur on a rabbit's back
summer by fly-struck sheep dying
drought by crazed marbling of mud in empty dams
flood by the brown sliding water in a river
taste by beer sliding over a tonsil
mothers by heat reflected warm as a mitten
life by the tough uncrackable leather of day labour
fathers by voices hard as a new saddle
death by the shiver of cats or a dog howling

Lay Day

I ride the tube
into a silence
of blue water
hinged to the axles
of the sea bed

on a wave that has travelled
a thousand miles to meet me
across storms and suns
Shark fin, whale fluke
hulls of ships
albatross wings
buried in it

star darkness
sunrise
Two miles out
the pitching lip breaks
into a breathless everness

I trim down
as the curl throws out
bend
test my own gravity
in the trawl and dredge
of a power-pack
big and gnarled as bondage

let a slew of waves
drag the stick in
left hand of the detonator

and write a million dollar day
in the sun's chequebook

The Sydney Harbour Club

At lunch hour the club dining room
serves balance sheets à la carte
with baked summer trout
followed by Blushing Apples
and Statistic Sauce
the J Line curves back on itself

Word goes round as to what phone jockey
is caught with his leg in the air
unable to complete a straddle
whether he needs a Bed-and-Breakfast deal
a daylight overdraft   a bullet loan
with the strike price aimed at a leap year
and what stale bulls
are dropping the All Ordinaries Index
on the new carpet
what bear jobbers riding a downturn

Roger waits in the club bar
    No I won't have a drink
    perhaps over lunch and thank you Sid

All his senses artificial horizons
tell him who's on level flight
what are the risks when the Bill-line tilts

The Minister glides past the doorman
his hand a shark's fin
slices the foyer in half
his smile shark sauce
to flavour a good lunch

    Ah there you are Roger
    Good to see you looking well
    I'll have oysters for my waist line

    and a bottle of Beaujolais
    so you can twist my arm
    in the right direction
    And now John about Greenville?
voice cool as a soft-loan lapping a factory site

Keep it under your napkin Roger
old man – it's looking good
The third Sydney airport *is* at Greenville
for all freight in and out
Better get on with the contracts
You were born there Know the place
You've got the vision
Buy the lot

The M6 swings backwards and forward
between oysters and coffee time
MICS and CHIPS and EFTS
are drawn down like dry Slutzkins
against ABS reports and Credit Lines
and questions whether
taking account of implicit price deflators
it's the right time to buy big-ticket items
lease them back
or stick to a butterfly spread
on the future's market
wait for multiplier effects

John you know there's a bar and a half
EFT to Switzerland for your eyes only
when the new zonings come in
Meanwhile before the number-crunchers pulverise Greenville
I'll get the options

By the end of the meal
seasonally adjusted farmers are ploughed in
yuppies gap black taxes with negative gearing
first home-loaners roost in housing statistics
old men shut their eyes on the Kondratieff cycles
sleep with upwardly mobile bellwether stocks
in the market where fat money eats the thin

Man into Sea

Coastlines of surfers
have grown into these latitudes
hunted Mega-waves
from Bell's Beach to Margaret River
classic points at Burleigh Heads   Noosa
Rincon   Huntington
The Pipe   Waimea

masters who broke down doors
Curren   Raging Bull
Swivel   Hero   Ace Cool
Big-wave riders
Nat Young   George Greenough
have cut skeg lines
on Thrusters   Flyers   beat-up guns
to become gurus of the ledge-break
groundswells from outer isobars

All Ordinaries Index

Driving home I follow the white line
past Neutral Bay houses
secrets in attics
TV screens watching the play
between possessor and possessed
armies audible in newsreaders' voices
men and women
clashing against one another

I switch on the radio
listen to the stock market
tie a ligature
on a company bleeding to death
crashed head on

No need to reconcile my speed
with exchange rates
that flick from red to green

In my own garage
I switch the Volvo off
near ledge-breaks
cradled in the Pacific's bed
nudging the coast below window lights
of expensive real estate

and not even at the sea's edge
will my own ambition
relinquish claims for adverse possession
nor those same waves
cross the concrete breakwater

Roger and the Stone of Heaven

The board rocks in the lift, fall and underwater swing on wave tangents that flow shorewards and they are to the sea what the motion of a great horse lifting his body over meadowlit mornings is to the land that slides under him when grass winds fall on valley shadows and hills lift him as high as a ridge crest so that he goes with the land-fall downwards on their curl over the clear lip to balance on the wind's face and feel how he is gathered up to become part of the world's run.

Trees next to his mane are Ming calligraphies, brush strokes made with mouse whiskers, unrecurring moments, each one taking a thousand days to paint from memory when mid-day has gone and his muscles are quiescent next to unbreathing shadows where ibis forage for insects as long as the sun is the colour of oxblood and the sky stretches to the far-off land of Serica and after storm the rainbow is a kingfisher.

Each wave passing under him furrows towards landmasses south into the beginnings of darkness undivided from unity with sky and sea, each one in harmony with boardriders who have gone out past white water to meditate for as long as the sun creaks, oiled water shifts and pauses while tides ring the changes so that they enter and are joined to every feature of the sea and the sea is meshed into their lives.

He reads lost words from the Book of Songs in waters smoother than silk tapestries. When he becomes the afternoon, sky-dragons with fiery tongues emerge from cloud banks and his own voice, a forked flame in the wind, sends shivers through The Tasman. He is a single note in a song played on a reed that has been forgotten for a long time but comes out of the wind's mouth of its own accord and is heard again.

The shore backwash is pure white porcelain. Clean abstract forms of gulls are held up to the sky, hidden figures in a Ming vase only visible against light.

He is a gold Bodhisattva more powerful than the water undulating under him, more magnificent than storms – in harmony with time to the vanishing point of all memory, myth, all legend, symbol of strength and power – centre of the universe and a special segment of each of its parts – moments that will never be repeated though waves become mountains of jade – and jade is the stone of heaven.

CHAPTER 2

GENERATIONS

The Whips and the Fathers

A mile out of town
the Killing Yards killed fat sheep
Fathers killed big blowy cows
hung hides on stringy-bark fences
Crows ate fat from dry pelts
Flies drummed in vats
where dripping was rendered
cut into square slippery blocks
trucked to the railway sheds

and over the hills
foxes put on red skins
killed rabbits and shiny dingos
killed white sheep in the night paddocks
Suns killed stars in the morning
scorched summer pastures in the afternoon
dried up the river
December killed silver carp
Black eels buried themselves in the mud
to avoid being killed
Fathers found them
and they too were killed

Sometimes the river broke free
but no father escaped nor the mothers
tied by wires of weddings and hardship
that wounded their kindness
for sons they bore and daughters
shut behind harsh closed windows
that knew darkness
better than it knew itself

The boy next door
had a father of iron
with a whip full of energy and spite
that taught dogs
to slur over the earth on their bellies
taught a horse to stand
tied to a fence for two days
killed every question the boy asked
punished him and the town

and the small river
swishing its tail painfully
all the way to the sea

He remembers fathers who flogged
clydesdales and ploughs through floodpans
September rains that softened the snake river
summers old as grandmothers' smiles
that dried up
eels, red foxes
his father's hard leathers
that would not be softened
by words his mother buried
in the mean town of weatherboard and sorrow
that let her die without dignity

High Country

There is an old gate
that needs to be opened again
locked against shooters
who would kill
the voice of a lyrebird
aim at any target
in all the silences

where Antill's Creek
joins the main stream
at the base of a she-oak
pulling its skirts off
as good a place to barbeque a steak
as anywhere on earth

where trees loft
against ridge and razorback
a wedgetail slides
into the wind's mouth
two three thousand feet up
north as far as Moorabak
south to the sky's end
where the noon plane
watches the gas line
right from Adelaide
and blue smoke
of fires we lit
warms a whipbird's call

I hear right now
a river half asleep
a wind inhale
while the old tree on the bank
pulls her shirt on
mad as a girl in love

nearby an old house
with a laugh no one can stop
I know its rooms and doors
I've said them a thousand times

the dog always at war
with strange footsteps

Generations

The western half of Greenville
swims to blue ranges
cattle and sheep-men herd

Drought ingrained in them
sucks dams and creek beds dry
Flood rains wash away profits

Truths of wedgetails
male female interlocked in mid air
meshed gears crossing light's bridges
skid down wild cumulus
weave and trawl a blue everness
angle every fall
to tilt flight sideways
swerve and cant inches from August suns

Anything is possible in Greenville

School Boys

When school came out
some of the boys went bush
to kill wood pigeons
larks and soldier birds

some fished to feel
silver carp and eels
with worms and bread
and fingertips

right until dusk
then set their lines
with grubs
and if I remember

few in particular
or too well
it is because
most were anonymous

others hot
as Elliot's bull
fought toe to toe
against God's will

or jerked themselves off
to see how far
white sperm tosses itself
who came first

and I the judge
stop watch slow
timed the contest
measured the throw

White Horse

Nareen was that child
on a white horse
quiet as a sleeping eyelash
who rode on velvet roads
to my house

In summer she was the blue feather
hidden in a contralto's voice

Inside her
quarrels of parents
who separated

One day the skylarks
were taken from the sky
The small horse broke a front leg
was shot

She tried to assemble a jigsaw puzzle
with parts missing

asked the landscape to accept her

Billy Tea

The day of dragonflies
we chose the smoothest rocks
in streams cool as a nurse's hand
the mountain's cowlick
just at the right angle
for two eagles
to massage the wind's scalp

I took riverwater
boiled warm light under candlebark
spooned in tea from Pakistan
a brew richer than summer's balance sheet

We drank dragonflies
sky
the mountain's curve
two eagles basted by the sun

Then left
counting blue coins
we took from the river's pocket

Mustering Cattle – Winter

This morning the wild boys are out
Fog too thick to see them

They play one side of the valley
against the other
strong voices
strong words
opinion straight from the gut

Those horsemen

covered in white milk
are only voices
Shorty Willis
and the Forester's son

It takes hours
for mist to rise
cattle to come in
sunlight's silver whip
to drive hills into sight

for Nareen
to stop singing
say
    I've never ridden
    better hills than these

Nareen Singing

Tonight liquid amber leaves
are husbands and wives

Who cares what they say
Stars dangle between your legs

apples
summer pears

arguing about the way
a north wind blows

only darkness between us
children with yellow hair

Roll down my stockings

Evan Green's Son

The boy next door walked awkwardly
moving his head backwards and forwards
with each step
a white hen with bright black eyes
an acquisitive boy with a hare-lip
a mother fat with affection
an icon for a father

The boy next door collected birds
recited their names as coloured poems
    flight detail   wing beat
    nest   egg shape
    instinct that brought them to town
    finches flycatchers sparrows
    breathless kingfishers
    wild kestrels of love
    passing from darkness to light

Each afternoon before sunset
carefully as a surgeon
he moved from tree to tree
catching honeyeaters
with his aiming eye
then down through snake grass
to collect red-backed wrens
by the pocketfull
fire opals blading willow leaves
cool as a mother's apron

Always at dusk
he dug small holes in the earth
emptied birds from his pockets
marked each with a pebble
too many to count
never good at maths
Then moving his neck like a hen
home to a father of iron
a mother warmer than gravy

CHAPTER 3

GREENVILLE

Reedy River

Greenville sleeps under songs of hymnmakers
of the left bank – a river
that has gone on to the granite coasts
and taken with it shadows of horsemen
who rode into legends
of fire and drought
or caught by floods
passed with brown snakes
down valleys that hide ancestors
under willows and histories
not written on scrolls
by delicate pens of scholars
nor passed on in dialects
of grandmothers and great aunts

The Municipal Council Chambers

A desultory clerk wakes up map cylinders
that have slept for years
under the Town Planner's sloping forehead

Roger makes himself uncomfortable
in a room where aldermen sit
to decide which Real Estate Agent
will profit from a DA
Spreads out a twenty year old plan
that shows grazing lands below western hills
where Farmer Anderson speaks to no one
not even the sheep
though his blue blood may be heard
to dynamite brittle arteries
and his bad joints creak in the frost

The township is hatched in autumn pastels
The pale Green Belt was belted into shape
to miss a prime allotment Alderman Green
had bought from a defaulting mortgagor
The Recreation Zone is red from football battles
Greenville fights with teams from nearby towns
and the Business Area painted light blue

He determines where an airfield will be viable
cross routes and flyovers for arterial roads
where an Industrial Corridor should open a fan
to cool debit entries on a cash-flow chart
what demands industry establishment will generate
the likely development costs of traffic snarls
and by rough arithmetic reworks
with the Mayor the risk factor

There is none

Lytton Street

Here among the small houses
winter again
This place has seen too many
since I left

Evan Green pensioner
shuffles through frost
sometimes snow
old boots
let in the cold like a guest house

The street named after a lord in England
who'd have none of it
a pain no one can cure
a tooth
one of the Greens
who can't afford a dentist
dabs on metho till the nerve is dead
a cough
doctored with honey
lemon juice
kerosene
remedies in these backyards
sterner than military law
whips guaranteed to buckle any back
starved sheep dogs
cars rustier than redemption
nowhere to go except backwards
not very far

Sometimes Jack Green
curses anonymous men at the top
who don't answer back
Neighbours shrug at his outbursts
but know he's right

Retired bricklayer
Every job he took ran at a loss
adds up to what he is
Blames governments
a war that set him back

Nights at the local pub with mates
puff his ego up
enable him to go home late
beat his wife
wake next day
tolerate her silence

Sees bad luck as part of the system
a race horse that leads to the straight
trips on a recessive gene
comes home last

Man into Clothesline

This is the grim backyard story
of Jack Green
a broken clothesline of a man
stained underpants
singlet never clean
handkerchief crying over a dog kennel
old socks shrunk by the washing machine
sheets from a double bed
thinner than muslin sunlight
that tries to bleach them

The paling fence of his life
defends an 8 square house
purchased 25 years back
from a salesman in a black suit
Borcelino hat
a package deal longer than any lifetime
mortgage from corporate stockholders
on the other side of the hill
who hold Jack Green
in a safe custody box

feeding a mongrel dog
credit foncier
wife Mary

rows of backyards
collateral to one another
every one in the street
signed sealed and delivered
mended and washed
pledged to Ace Securities Inc.
in a deed box
that will remain locked
for 25 years at least

Number 23 Lytton Street

No. 23 was on the wrong side of the road
It had been that way a long time
Vacant   all the windows out of focus
fences with broken arms
A place where schoolboys came
to kill black snakes
take starlings from nests under eaves
wring their necks

When rainy October was dripping through the roof
a man wrapped tightly in his middle age
unlocked the door with a wife's efficient hands
mowed the grass
disposed of plastic bags
westerlies had stolen from the town dump
killed the last of the snakes

Jack Green came by   said good day
The man didn't answer and his wife smiled
A peregrine falcon stooped
to snatch a mouse from newly mown grass
was shot with the wink of an eye

When Jack said the street was a bird sanctuary
the man blew smoke from a gunbarrel
didn't say a word
Not on speaking terms with anyone
intended to keep it that way

All the work he did improved nothing
The house remained as ugly as Jack's wife
uglier in fact
scuffing around the yard
cross-bred bitch
Growled at everyone who passed

Another falcon visited the wrong side of the road
A wink and it too died

One afternoon without warning
cages were brought in

hundreds of them
Suddenly No. 23 was a city
blue and red with gallinaceous birds
plumage laced with black
pheasants from Japan and China
silver   yellow   orange
ringnecks and tragopans
One bright Mongolian
partridges from America and Greece
bob whites   red-legs
small twisted quail
hazel grouse

Birds shrieked mating calls
to savannahs in distant lands
Thailand   Mongolia   Pakistan
The world was upside down
all Asia in Lytton Street

Often thin calls
hunted the earth before dawn
searching for eastern suns
A golden pheasant escaped
lived with Jack's cats
burning India into a violet patch
touching low shrubs with velvet

Every Thursday night
a shrill chorus of birds
woke Lytton Street
Jack asked the birdman why
and could he take a look
No answer
A half smile from the wife

Jack shut the gate on the way out
and waited up one night
to watch the shed back of the house
birdman and wife at work
cutting bright throats
and her red hands
plucked ringnecks and tragopans
stipped bob whites
twisted quail

loaded a freezing van
marked Game Birds Inc.
Took the world from the street

The birdman left
as quietly as he came in
The small houses returned to their grim looks
No. 23 invited the snakes back
starlings to build nests under the eaves
asked schoolboys to climb the fences
break their necks

Only a golden pheasant remained
lived with friendly cats under a gorse bush
image warm
against the suns of Raznapur
and in the winter violets
on warm July days

Andronicus Green

Andronicus Green is building a yacht in his front garden
and this town's above the snowline
a hundred kilometres from the sea
The street's farther away than that

It doesn't matter to Mr Green
The ten metre hull slices his lawn in half
keel in couch grass
prow nosing the white chrysanthemum bed

Each afternoon he climbs aboard
wears a captain's hat
and from the level deck
charts shores of distant lands
hunts whale packs north and south of Capricorn
anchors in harbours blue as a kelpie's eye
and though he rarely drinks
brawls through brothels and pubs
from Rio to Mersey Side

then begins the midnight shift
at the meat works on top of the hill
admits he's the knife sharpener

cuts the throat of every day in his life
slashes stomach walls of billowy cows
anchored by hocks to chains on moving belts
severs perineum, mesentary membrane
wades through Sargassoes of guts
to open rib cages
that teach him how to brace the white hull
on his front lawn
then swings each carcass hulk to the next man

Back in Lytton Street
he puts on the captain's hat

goes below like Ahab
for forty winks
while Mrs Green his Moby Dick
baleens among the chrysanthemums

and the keen bow slits rain and sleet
in the Ross Sea
where even the sun shivers

Winter '85
spent the last of his daylight at the Seafarer's Arms
and rolling drunk
cursed schoolboy deckhands
all the way down Lytton Street
and back on the for'ard deck
looked at the uncompromising sea

Whales spouted off the leeward beam
With one clean stroke
he harpooned the biggest in the pack

That was Mrs Green
who blew and sounded in her garden bed
Fought ropes that tightened on him
grips harder than pack-ice
dragged him under the waterline with unbreakable force
that teaches every man to live and die

Police from some flea-bitten port
near Santa Cruz
blind to intricacies of shipbuilding and the sea
untangled knots under the clean hull
spat a few words
on the bitter wind blowing up from the south

The Church on the South Bank

Misereatur vestri omnipotens Deus
et dimissis peccatis vestris.

Today the sun is rich as America
full of warheads
Tourists bristle dollar bills
Big semis hell-bent for Melbourne
wipe out speed signs
as they tip their hats to Evan Green's house
that nudges the north bank

It's the kind of day
to write to relatives
complain about food prices
read editorials that predict nuclear war
telephone bank managers for overdrafts
That's what Evan does
in a front room full of sepia dust
and silences

At St Francis Xavier's Roman Catholic Church
old Mrs Parkes mumbles
Agnus dei, qui tollis
pecátta mundi, miserére nobis
No one hears
Not even God

The loud voice of Father Ahearn
leading the choir
drowns out everything
except schoolboys
trying to kill a king parrot
bad tempered bird
beak sharper than taxes
but when he flies off
his big flashy red V8
fires the wind
Hi Fi system
playing rock music full blast

Then only the voice of Father Ahearn
crosses the river
singing to Evan Green
    A bird of the air
    shall carry my voice

and this is any country in the world

A song no one will ever know

in the distance
happy and sad
Suddenly no conflict
no threat of war

A long way off
Russia is whistling
Reagan shooting it out
at Dead Man's Gulch
while Father Ahearn
puts the convincer on God

    Time and chance happeneth to them all
    For man knoweth not his time
    and the fishes are taken in an evil net

Carat is any Colour

That bower bird has no tax problems
knows more about fiscal drag
than the Prime Minister
Could criticise the system
better than any man
Only thing
he can't resist any object coloured blue
old beads
bits of plastic
a toothbrush
arranged carefully in his bower
like statute books
He'd pull down the sky
and slap the sea
in the middle of his nest

He's different from crows and magpies
on a golf course
Greg Norman or The Golden Bear
shooting the best drive in the Rothmans
The ball lands near the pin
easy as helicopters
Crow dives in
takes the white egg of that strange cargo cult
to the top of the highest tree on the fairway

That's of no importance to a bower bird
but where there's a hint of blue
he's a lawyer homing in on a fat divorce
a doctor hooked to a brain tumour
or one of the really big corporations
winning a government tender
to build a launching site
by flicking a million dollars haphazardly
into the Party's slush fund
or shaking hands with tumblers
in a Swiss bank account
numbered by the Minister's *best friend*

That bower bird is a big man
red as February
strolling about in a balance sheet

to catch cash-flows off guard
expense accounts
percentages
and lay down blue-sky laws
to snatch green dollars from graphic plans
and micro chips
watch computer runs
arrange a plastic life in clever ways
when all the logic's gone

build wild jigsaw puzzles
from any blue object in the blue world

Jack Green's Great Aunt (Matilda Rowley Parkes)

Old Mrs Parkes died a thousand times

At midnight she died for the last time
Only the full moon was awake
laughing at snow clouds
that skidded across the highway heading south
It didn't say anything
to her eldest truckdriver son
mauling a big road freighter
towards Melbourne

Her youngest son was killed on a night like this
a car smash   too much alcohol
Mrs Parkes died for the first time
buried her sorrowing face in a photograph
with a silver frame

Then followed a husband's suicide
A grandfather's death   Her favourite cat
Others she memorised over ninety years
like prayers whispered into a limp handkerchief

Her last death was on the toilet seat
in the third son's house
knees braced against a door that opened inwards
a wedge all grandmothers need
Her son axed it down

Old Mrs Parkes slid quietly to one side
giving way to everything close to her
face sad as a codicil
purple from the waist down
blood drained into old legs
that in their time had walked useless miles
through the mean streets in this town

The Croesus Cement Company

Evan Green pensioner
retired cement worker, age fifty three
lives in No. 11
coughing up dust
from thousands of days
shift-working in the
iron light of economic theories
that twisted his back
bending down to lift sour gypsum
he had no wish to touch

The company gave him a generous loan
part of the work package
a rate of interest better than
money in the bank
suited a married man
with thirty years to liquidate
and a contract with no let-out clause
signed on the poverty line

The end of his working life
was served on the company's slag heap
planting stunted trees
afraid to put roots down
into the black ground

The owners of Croesus Cement
never visited him
where TV aerials suck programmes
from the southern sky
gently as tax plans

Nevertheless they know
the jewels in a Statement of Assets
dividends are always high
Evan's life amortised
over thirty years it takes
to pay a mortgage back
and in their subtle way
have written that ordinary man
into the All Ordinaries Index

CHAPTER 4

REDEVELOPMENT PLANS

Collectables

Prices have gone up
but Roger easily buys the Green Belt
Open Spaces that have always been open
the bowling club
where old men bend over bad hearts
and sometimes say good-bye to a friend

Within six months he has the town
in a Christmas grip
and the Town Planner
frowning over a Redevelopment Plan

The powerful Left have been promised
their profit in kiss or kind
The Mayor blinks at his new bank balance
Everyone who matters is on the right side
pressing the Minister to approve
rezonings he'd already agreed with Roger
in the Club dining room
where all great enterprises and their collectables
pass through the pilot stage.

Zackery Green

Seasons judge this old man
going one day at a time
at exactly ten o'clock
two four-pronged walking sticks
Not in a hurry to go anywhere
nor to return
Winter and summer
excessive weights
strapped on his back
carried past electric light poles
in this street
which does not begin nor end
tailored to fit him exactly

First the left stick lifted
pushed forward
lowered
thigh jerked to follow it
hip, back, head
levered to begin a balancing trick
right stick lunged
to defy gravity
rock the world in slow motion

Nobody knows the beginning of his journey
where it will end
He is in one place at a time
a calisthenics of joint pains
One stick at a time
covers his shadow
touches the ground
to check if it's still there
verify it

Budget Account

In the words of Bob Ansett
"Perception is reality"

Already Acme Grinding Co
and Merlin Transmutation Inc
have fed Greenville to the computers
made rude forecasts of population movements
decided to build smoke shadows across Lytton Street
that will change the blur of old walls
into sharply defined silhouettes of factories
A fast-food company predicts in chicken days
how many need be killed
to feed appetites plucked from Cartesian co-ordinates
on a demand graph

Greenville knows nothing of Trans Asian Finance Inc
the Jewish money-dealer in New York
Sheik Abdul Mumtaz Begum with oil reserves
and a sinking fund in Eurodollars
that will surely sink Greenville
nor of Mr Wong's connection with The China Bank

Evan Green saved for his old age with the Commonwealth
Jack's wife saves Jack's underpants by ritual stitching
Honeysuckle wins its battle with Andronicus
by twisting roof-guttering into sailor's knots
Zackery counts days in The Year of The Heart Attack
They do not number 365

Mr Wong adds an intercalary month
to The Year of The Pig
while the Mayor dreams in his scrotum
of catching young girls and Mako sharks off South Head
with the money he'll get – and Mary
prays for forgiveness of sins she'll never commit

The Expectancy Life Insurance Company
decides what death benefits it will sell to the Greens

Andronicus Green's Thought Patterns

These mountains quivered last night
Was it drought
shrinking barbed distance
Earth making love
Some old fox with a green vixen
testing his penis
learning it works well
on an empty stomach

or bulldozers
finishing the freeway cloverleaf
under arc-lights
so the Minister can keep his promise
to tired voters

I thought of these possibilities
the fox's penis
the Minister testing his foreskin
on the electorate
a policy speech
rubbing the night's crutch
antique beds in tune
with an empty-belly-rock beat

From my own house
it's possible to throw a stone
break windscreens of big trucks
going south
through the vulva of a white bridge
while the river scribbles a codicil to history

Who gives a damn
about answering difficult questions
By mid morning the cryptorchid sun
will polish my old tom cat
with feral light

Father O'Brien's Sermon to Skylarks

Laudate Dóminum omnes gentes

1986 8AM
Satellites tell Australia
Beirut is dying
Cricket scores replayed
defy credibility
Nato forces practise war games
learn to survive
tomorrow's nuclear attack

These brown birds could tell the generals
a thing or two

My own room
is an untidy battlefield
papers everywhere
books on the floor
The keyboard yawns
sermon unfinished
left hand asleep

It is a pleasant thing
for my eyes to behold the sun

Outside the sky's parachute
fills with skylarks
Invisible against the light

and I shall rise up
at the voice of the birds

Songs fall like banknotes
on the wind's eyelash
brushing the first day of spring
telling the world
summer is inches away

Laudate Dóminum omnes pópuli

The Fast Lane

I drive past lighted windows
and there is nothing to say
to the woman who draws her blinds
against the sea wind
shuffling in from the harbour
nor to the man whose dog life
pisses on gates neighbours
shut with philosophies
plaited from various unmatching strands
they manage to weave
into a lead that secures them
to whatever hand tugs
bodies past buildings
where they need to cock a leg
and at least leave some mark
to let the world know
they've been

My mind is stuffed
with the memory of these streets
so that my arms twist exactly
at the reflex of each intersection
twice every day
on the way into the square
thought-chamber I call office
and back to the bed
my wife accepts
sometimes dangerously close
to accident
mostly with the same reflex
with which a car is driven
on a road map
not needing to be read
on a bad night
where mercury lights
glare down on the fast lane
and one body overtakes another
simply to get off it

CHAPTER 5

BLUE DYNAMITE

The new Silk Road

Leaving the tax storms of Australia
the jumbo jet steers through
southern winter
The equator's speed-hump
hardly rocks the first-class passenger lounge

Roger swallowed 2 Mogadons at take off
with a double Armagnac
sleeps on the glass surface of chemical twilight
towards fiscal sunshine in Hong Kong
where lawyers and tax consultants
turn profits to non-assessable gains
through a chain of caterpillar companies
that crawl past tax commissioners
and on clear brainstorming days
are visible from Victoria Peak to Liechtenstein

Blue Dynamite

The Boeing slid into Kai Tak Airport
The Shangri-La Hotel nodded when Roger entered
    Yes Mr Nosegay has reserved a suite on the 20th level
    Please wait sir your luggage is being attended to
The crowded reception desk
tugged at the Manager's coat sleeve

A girl new as Brasilia
looked at herself in the foyer wall mirror
Eurasian skin the colour of pale apricots
Issey Miyake gear sharp as year two thousand
jade moiré silk shading to sea mirage

To Roger she was a Lamborghini Quattrovalvole
crashing red lights in the noon rush-hour
with the power to cross language-barriers without speaking

The mirror looked back at eyes
pastel shadowed with Cendre d'Or
Mauve d'Orange
lips Perle Fauve by Polished Perfection
a necklace of Biwa pearls with emerald front piece
on the right finger a single loupe-clean diamond

She stepped into the ascending lift with Roger
The music of shoes ceased when she stopped walking
Two husbands looked away from wintery wives
The lift slid quietly to the tenth level and stopped
She glanced at Roger eyes blue as dynamite
The half smile on her lips polished performance

Behind her lift doors closed against inscrutable graphics

40% of the Action

In Nosegay & Partner's conference room
Roger approves the cost plus carpet
suede leather walls
gold light, antiques, painted ships
No dusty bureaucrats in their filing cabinets
A free exchange market
tax scale in low range
The partners already have the tax brief
and from his attaché case Roger takes
the map that unsuspecting Greenville
is about to become
drops a cash flow chart and a Minister's name
onto the mahogany table
Nosegay Junior swishes his tail
The senior partner wags a tax structure
that twitches like an ejaculation
discretionary trust
tax taken to account as an operating cost
more soothing to clients than post coital sleep

    Already I've warmed Mr Wong's backside
    on the gold chair of the conference room
    and he'll joint venture for 40% of the action
    His own company set-up is in position
    You'll need to bathe in the fiscal waters
    of Queen's Road for a while
    sip afternoon tea in the shelter of the Peninsula's verandah
    escargots a la Bourguignonne at Pierrot's Restaurant

        I'd rather reserve a table for dinner at Gaddi's
        dial for a hostess a hundred and sixty three centimetres tall

    My son will ring Mr Wong
    who will arrange everything to your liking –
    while we incorporate
        Greenville Offshore Fund
            ,,   Buttressing Differential
            ,,   Exempt Accruals
            ,,   External Benefits
            ,,   Charity and Retirement Fund

and a Service Company in Singapore
    Greenville Haven & Security Inc.
as well as all the agreements
and get some cash up-front from Mr Wong

We'll sell short   buy long
start things rolling while the bears are in
antiques, paintings, ships
Even a divorced wife won't know what you own
There's no tax on switching assets here
No Section 25A
that's hunted your countrymen from Jones versus Leeming
down through McLelland's case
and left them high and dry
when the tide ebbed sadly under the High Court
on Whitford Beach

That can't happen to you with Discretionary Recovery
and Reversionary Windfall Inc
You won't become a refugee from political intervention
in private monetary gains

Back at the Shangri-La
Roger watches container barges
cross the water
sampans switch tourists at Star Ferry Wharf
visiting seagulls balance on the harbour

Late afternoon he opens his door
to a girl
new as Brasilia
eyes blue as dynamite

I am
one hundred and sixty three centimetres tall
My name is Eveline

The Power Pack

I am as I am and cannot put the entrails
of the ancients into my own belly

– Ho Li Wong

Mr Wong left the Smoke Stack industries
for finance twenty years ago
His house rides the highest price-ticket
on Victoria Peak
His private quarters a hall of Supreme Harmony
with bronze guards
who still measure time in Dynastic cycles

After a morning spent managing risk
his wife in robes of a sleeve dancer
remembers with him the Streets of Heaven
under the flame of a fire-gilded lamp
in the shape of a sacred ram
and the flicker of silk lightning

He's back to the risk-reward ratio
always looking for a window to climb in
examining deals in a matrix
that shuffles the venture capital market
through 75 man-years of software
balance sheets whose only assets
are intellectual property
a data-base on information management
that redenominates currencies of exposure
and tells him not to deal in basket wampum
and what debt management programme
he'll need to cover the *what if* scenarios
Roger's project postulates

Eveline

The Bank of Hong Kong slid easily under Mr Wong
as easily as the AUS dollar slipped
into the wide ocean trench of Ho Li South
China Sea Finance Company's accounts
as easily as Greenville would vanish
without leaving a trace of Zackery
or Matilda Rowley's leathery face
or Farmer Anderson whose acres covered an oil basin
wider and deeper than the Yellow River in flood
as easily as Roger's pen would slide
over Nosegay's mortgage documents
and he in turn had slid into the graceful logic
of Tao and over ground swells
that hung from other worlds at Angourie and Rincon
where he entered the third reality

as easily as Eveline in turn slid under him
skin the colour of light apricots
a design not visible in strong sunlight

Golden Plover

Twenty floors above the money dance
my tongue learns new dialogues
from your skin

When your name falls across me
not one vowel or dipthong
lies between us

Your eyelashes are ferns
in a rainforest
and I need to speak low in you

I rinse you in my mouth
move into you
with the energy of Arabs
slide down the long corridors
of your body
cross the bridge between thigh and elbow
to the secret hallways of your feet

I am a boardrider
near the island in your eyes
who swings through his own stance
across the face of a wave
that detonates
on the flange of a reef

Then I am hand in your rock

Eveline's Lyric

I am the geisha in your underwear
the punk-rocker on disco floors
Kiri Te Kanawa singing Maria
in West Side story
the force driving racehorses and Ferraris
a lift gliding to the fiftieth level

I am the wind's whisper before storms
the lyric in your arm's vice

My shoes sing through the streets
My bare feet make music on your carpet

Day Dress

In the foyer of the Mandarin
you are that tall woman
leaning against my breath
who walks through her own garments
into ordinary speech

You stroll down Connaught Road
towards the bay
a sail in bronze
that loves all the Trade winds

The braille of your skin
warms my hands
and I kneel beside your face
silent in the valleys
your voice creases

Eurasian

Eveline glided through the darkness of Kowloon
in a red Porsche Targa that curved through traffic
as gracefully as a mako shark off Freshwater
Roger in the passenger seat stroked the inside
of her left leg the colour of pale apricots

She had two weapons always at the ready

a body where East met West in celestial harmony
a mind like the third eye of Buddha
taught Roger unearthly pleasures
and the arts of love

He talked of mega crests at Maui and Rincon

Hours merged with seascapes of boardriders
at Bell's Beach and those where he was alone
on the sea's freight trains turning the rail
into ground swells, trimming a gun board's tail
on a tube's shoulder to cut-back
into big Blue Birds running in from the east

A Fung Shui man examined Roger's right hand
    You are a true Taoist. May you always
    enjoy the seven Golden Pleasures

At the Royal Jockey Club race meeting they won
seven thousand dollars on a horse named Geomancer
Roger gave her perfume and kisses of honey agate
He was a new breath in her lung's alveoli

Each night she opened the windows of The Milky Way

Roger's Love-Song

You are the delicate craft in Ming Dynasty vases
love-day longer than Arctic summer

I am a bell in your body's carillon
clock in rhythm with your heartbeat

Segovia's fingers on a guitar
in the Court of Lions at the Alhambra

I am all the suns of Australia
a shofa calling from North Sinai
across Akaba to the Red Sea
snow-water from the Sierra Nevadas
melting into the Guadalquivar

I am the torch
she said
what to me
if the moth die of me?

– Eveline

The Lion and the Dragon

At Nosegay & Partners the business
was slowly done – Mr Wong
has digested cash-flow charts
forecasts of growth, industry acceptance
graph-scales of market surveys
spread-sheets
oncost effectiveness
    Honeywell said Exchange rates
    follow a random walk and since this is
    a stand-up situation *hedge the risk*
    The business cycle will peak
    like a coolee hat
    through the fiscal policy of the Labour Party

Nosegay's whiskers quivered
the junior partner gave away a half smile
quickly took it back
Roger remained quiet as a memóry bank
    Hewlett-Packard said
    The strike price of forward currencies is back
    Buy a call-option to hedge risk exposure
    Lock in the cost of payables and so on
    through USD's, Euro and multi-currency loans
    break-even rates on DEM's

so that Greenville became a mix
of call and put, Debt management
mixed with the shade of elm trees falling
across July when one Green dies
or where December opens its eyelids
when another is born

and though world currencies like Alcoholics Anonymous
move one day at a time
in cycles as varied as a Greenville year
the no-risk factor when a Green
fires sperm cells into an egg bank
needs neither philosophy nor insurance
to cover the end-result

Greenville listens to many languages

Ten agreements marched across the table
a banquet only Nosegay Senior could prepare
Junior twitched from room to room
sorting *what-if's* all lawyers devise

Mr Wong would money-manage the venture
Roger, predisposed to win
would roll Greenville like a roulette wheel
when the banker calls *rien ne va plus*
backed up by multi-corporate structures
that would tease any liquidator
who tried to peep behind the corporate veil

Questions of domicile
lex loci contractionis
shook hands with Halsbury Volume 10
The All England Law Reports
issued bland judgements
with impeccable Oxford accents
confirming that the ratio decidendi
of Lord Mornington's dictum
and all the precedents of the High Court
of Australia and Hong Kong
had been taken into account

Only when the documents were properly sealed and delivered
did Nosegay & Partners contribute another half-smile
and this one they didn't take back

Mr Wong Holds a Banquet

Today only a wealthy man can function as an individual
the poor and the bourgeoise are a collective mass hardly
distinguishable one from another.

– Ho Li Wong

Mr Wong's house on Victoria Peak
a rich ornament, hung from columns
surrounded by a silence that may only be crossed
by winds blowing in from the China Sea
or rainstorms that tumble through cyclonic depressions
move westwards along low isobars
and sweep quickly towards The New Territories

Nosegay Junior arrived at the exact minute
The Senior Partner followed after a discrete interval
each of their wives
contained within the Rule against Perpetuities
bound by limitations of a trust for life
entered the Hall of Supreme Harmony
where Mr Wong said *May you rejoice and grow rich*
Mrs Wong delicate as a silk painting from the third millenium
added *Welcome. Put on greater prosperity*

The lights of Kowloon shone through the glass east wall
and Mr Wong's pool
reflected The Dynasty of Aquarius

Below The Connaught Centre blazed, the Bank of Hong Kong
and on the sixtieth level, The Office of The White Bird

Tides slip into Victoria Harbour
like visitors who do not stay too long
Roger sank into the Tai Po carpet alone
Nay Ho Ma he bowed to Mrs Wong

Servants poured Shaohsing wine from a Ho
cast when Shang-Yin ruled Serica

Peace settled over the small group
the marvellous flying grass of Ming calligraphies

a poem by Tu Fu on the west wall
recording in brocade a village that came unstitched
fine wheat and the Magistrate of Kou-Lou
who displeased the poet
lacquer screens and eight porcelain bowls
in gray-green celadon, red copper glaze
iron yellows from The Third Dynasty
jade plugs from a burial ground
one from the anus of a dead King
one from a servant's mouth
and a long slim needle-plug that fits the eye of a penis

Eveline entered the room
dressed in a sheongsam red for happiness
Mr Wong smiled with an inner meaning
      I believe you already know my grand-daughter
and Roger was lost in the surprise
of a painting on silk in ink and colour

Tiger losing his winter coat near a bamboo lodge
against frost on distant mountains
by an unknown artist

      I didn't know she was your grand-daughter

and next to the swimming pool visible through glass doors
the garden balanced the delicate relationships
that existed between men, nature and Mr Wong

Eveline, a pheasant – emblem of the sun –
swayed against tapestries and hand scrolls
of misty valleys   The stillness of an Oriental hand
resting on his life briefly
a pleasure natural as breath
a Tao scroll of the second reality

At 9pm the party left for the Banquet Hall
at the Restaurant of The Three Kingdoms

In The Room of Tranquility Mr Wong thanked Nosegay Senior
for anchoring Greenville in a tax haven
while listing delicacies of Chinese culinary art
Lady in the Cabbage, Drunken Chicken from Shanghai and
Ningpo

Ants on The Tree from Szechuan, Sizzling Rice Soup
Plum Blossom in Snow competing for Spring
Spun Apples from the north
explaining that each course should come from the same region
Delicate Oo-long and Plum Chiew wines
Desserts Pa Pao Fan, Yen Wo T'ien T'ang

Observing Mr Wong Roger looked at the surface
of a bottomless lake on which no Occidental might swim
watched him devour every morsel
remembered the jade plugs
one from the anus of the dead king
in The Hall of Supreme Harmony

The bronze Buddha at the entrance laughed
The shark fin motif in flung ink shimmered
Nosegay settled deeper into his Corpus Juris

A feast is made for laughter
Wine maketh merry:
but money answereth all things.

– Sir Dalrymple Nosegay.

CHAPTER 6

SCREW RULES AND DRIFT RATES

Progress

Six months have intervened
between the first and last step
like a lawyer between litigants

Andronicus Green is foreman
of The Acme Grinding Company
which grinds away day after day
but never ejaculates
The yacht weathers quietly in the chrysanthemum bed
as does Andronicus' wife
Not one puff of his wind
will fill her sails again
When he comes home he's too tired
to play Ahab with a rusty harpoon
and she always has a headache

The Airfield runway is half finished
Expectancy Life Insurance Co
has scattered generous death benefits like ashes
into work-related illness
and the doctors wait for the next
generation of patients
to go out the same way

High rise flats have dimmed elm light
Each has a Chinese name
Mr Wong chose from The Book of Forgetfulness
Some of the old houses have been sawn in half
by Evan Junior
attached to prime movers
driven to Bull Ant Spur
where Mary has taken her clothes hoist
like a Jesus-cross and Jack has gone along

The F6 Freeway south
dissects the best grazing property
below western hills
once owned by Squatter Anderson
who can't squat anymore
He still speaks to no one
though his bad bones creak
and his blue blood continues to dynamite brittle arteries

He who seeks equity must do equity
though the Merlin Trust & Transmutation Co
bit Evan Green in half on the courtroom floor
where he almost bled to death
while impartial Mr Justice Furore
tied a ligature of soothing words
above the wound and on moral grounds
dusted them with an order
that Merlin pay its own costs

The Mayor disguised as Okam Krahs Ltd
caught the big one
and bought a luxury penthouse at Pearl Bay
a cruiser and a Benz
He visits Greenville occasionally
with a hostess painted on the passenger seat
and his britches stuffed full of bank notes
to tame bureaucrats
and steer semi-government autocracy
through dangerous shallows

Hewlett-Packard
gives him the good oil
he rubs into whatever needs lubricating

Burroughs Wong and IBM

Zackery's walking stick
twitches at 10am daily
moves into Zackery's right hand
without assistance
guides him to the Public Bar at The Beer Tank
It knows the exact level
to which his Social Service sinks each day
and when sufficient is spent it jumps quickly
onto his palm leaving enough for tomorrow
guides him past the Celestial Flats
to the old house that keeps out wind and rain

while the Safardic Jewish Money-broker in New York
who'd studied at Yashiva
celebrates Rosha Shana thinking quietly
to himself of Australia
which thank God he'll never visit
and sings in a Brooklyn accent
    Baruch ata adernoi elahamu
and thank God touch wood he'll never need
to kiss Mr Wong
in The Hall of Celestial Moneylenders

The shadows of elms
are cut by imprints of superstructures
in prestressed post-tensile concrete
sharp as shark's dorsal fins
The town dump will become a Sport Centre
and Community Amenities Block

Tokyo graduates test the waters of an Industrial Heaven
Japanese businessmen in Pierre Cardin suits
watch Zackery and Father O'Brien
with bemused intolerance

Migrants are moving in
all Asia putting Greenville on the map

Only the night sky is Aldebaran's province
Not even Mr Wong can mortgage the stars
take leasehold estates on interstellar space
nor over light years
that sparkle on a brief timespan
then go out
though Burroughs Wang and IBM
are working on it

Riding the Groundswell

When Sydney is waking
I straddle board and horizon
move into the second of the set
coasting on the swell

then break the trim line
turn and use the rail lightly
close to fall
over the curl
bend knee for recoil
weight towards face
to the end of this arc
cross the lip
into the open sea
stroll on to the next
big screamer
top turn and run down fall
on a pivot and break out

before the detonator
explodes at my feet

Antiglare Monitor

In Mr Wong's office of The White Bird
the electroluminescent display
set next to an ancient digital abacus
flicks over differential interest rates
as if it had touched oracle bones
from the Shang Period
or the magic jade fish
that never die
whatever draw-down dates
slip through a purchasing parity theorem
to prove the waters are warm in Switzerland
or it's just the exactly right minute to buy
a forward exchange contract in Deutsche Mark

and after an afternoon reading documents
prepared by Nosegay & Partners
under hanging scrolls in ink and light colours
on silk and the one he likes most

Fighting oxen with tails pressed between their legs
by Kuo-Jo-Liu ii

he covers the main agreement
with a dagger axe
he's used as a paperweight
for twenty years

Letter from Hong Kong

Your body
names every part of the night
from one edge to the other

Now in the darkness
clothes on my chair
remember your smooth skin

I tell you with the flesh of my tongue
I wish you were here
to grow into my earth

shadow and fall
as abstract as your measure
and there's many a way
to measure you

You are golden thorns of ideograms
stitched into the silk neon lights
of Harcourt Road

There's nothing here
to fill the emptiness
in the leaves of my still hands

I need your shape
to gather itself against me

Eveline

The Big Rhino

I take my gun-board into the surf-zone
roll under the stick in the close-outs
oyster-smell a world of patterns and noise
past Two Mile Reef

Peaks ledge at the north headland
Left handers
If I beat the curl
work the face south
there's a chance
don't get wiped out

The biggest mother in a set takes me
and I take her
clean off the lip
into the power zone
She roars and spits me out
I wall on my knees to miss a tunnel
then on the speed-line
free-fall down the face
I'm stoked to the point of burn-out
tough as Rambo
eating it up
I'm in and power plus
suckers on my feet

Nothing can throw me
It's my wave now
I hold the ridge again
going for it close to the pocket
past the bombora
stoned off my face
hooting in the roar of backward verticals
Got it wired
don't hear any voice
The stick shivers on a ledge
nearly snaps
hangs on

The Music of Metal and String Instruments cannot match the Song of a Silk Dress

The 747B skimmed the cream off the sky
Eveline sat in the first class passenger lounge
glanced idly at a line-chart of currency alternatives
Homebase had shaken hands with Barnhoff Strasse
through SOPHONET to mainframe
read the future of Greenville like a Fung Shui man

The sun struck matches on Sydney Harbour
Qantas tossed wind over its shoulder
skyscrapers nudging Circular Quay
The city lay under the port wing like a nest egg
linked by fibre optics to every other city on earth
Honeywell and IBM swapped tall stories in laser language
of coups brought off in Castlereagh Street
Ferries graphed inlets and quiet bays
while Roger waited at the terminal

He kissed Eveline harder than a jade bodhisattva
The New Hilton Hotel turned over in bed
Greenville snored quietly to the west
Roger inhaled a fragrance that will last 1000 years
stroked the benign mole on her left buttock
hair blacker than manganese
the inside of her leg the colour of pale apricots

They visited Greenville under the elm light
of old trees hatched red on the new map
flight paths cargo-jets would follow
in an out of the Lytton terminal the Mayor
had bought and sold at the right price
Eveline tested her flow-chart in Reedy River
where schoolboys drew yabbies out of hiding

Armed with a degree in Computer Sciences
from Stanford University
and a period of meditation at Rothschild's Bank
she was more than a match for ageing widows

Compared acquisition costs with poverty levels
hidden under the iron roofs of Lytton Street

checked graph contours against gentle grasslands
watched Roger on the fall-line of wave sets at Yowie Bay
searched him for all the clues he had hidden
found the lot – slipped them into her memory bank
to retrieve when grandfather
might need to put him away
As Mr Wong's dagger hand she had struck many times
with eyes cold as inner rooms of derelict houses

The day before she left for Hong Kong
Roger introduced her to his mother
who was always asleep at South Head Cemetry
and through the silent summer afternoon
they watched sea mirages and a Mako shark,
"blue dynamite", did a U-turn against the sky
cleared the surface by twenty feet

He said goodbye to the longest day in his life
when he drove Eveline to Mascot International Airport
where jumbos snored on the tarmac before takeoff
farted and blew their trumpets at Roger
turned north on the new Silk Road to the Orient

CHAPTER 7

THE J CURVE

Black Gold

Mr Wong scans The Dow Jones News Retrieval Service
daily The Source, Compuserve
through programmatic chains from Link to Host
after setting the password on the DSN workstation
to transmit files in flexible syntax
designed to mesh with Nosegay & Partner's clauses
tax structures Commissioners can't dismantle
batch-access capacities to perform
time-slotted projects on Greenville's rough terrain
modify configurations of side-streets
redefine the terminator character
on escalating work-force postulates
then smiles an Oriental smile of satisfaction
in his office of The White Oriole
and sips shark-fin soup between courses
at The Imperial Lo Han Chai Restaurant

Tom Green and old Mrs Parkes
do not care that the blue mountains westwards
are smudged with factory smoke and legal ink
that Greenville Coal Enterprises
have diamond-drilled their sleep

Minerals not reserved to The Crown
in the original Grant belong therefore to Mr Wong
and his Hall of Celestial Sleep
Already he's negotiated contracts with Egypt
on a scale in the ratio of 1:1000
to transport even their bones if necessary
from a coal-loading facility
that covers the best beach on the nearby coast

Father O'Brien's flock has diminished
to a trickle behind the church on the south bank
though his voice can better be heard
admonishing old ladies who have never sinned
Trees have given way to a subdivision
Bulldozers have moved earth
neither God nor Father O'Brien could shift

Zackery Remembers Old Greenville

Elms dragged noon shadows in from the sun
Vines crept under honeyeaters like caperpillars
Ploughs turned over the pages of summer grass
Dossiers of rain were never audited

Children lagged behind old men
Deaths, marriages and trains were always late
Summer dawns sometimes rose at 5 o'clock
sometimes 9
depending which of the Greens
needed to get out of bed
or whether it was Sunday

Slow Parish Registers drawled through 100 years
a language we did not understand

A dialect not suited to hard disks
that store bit-mapped images
in extension slots
nothing like Pascal MT86 or Fortran

Not even on crutches
could Old Greenville reach year 2000 on time

Floating the Dollar

Who can blame a eunuch
for not having a beard

– Ho Li Wong

When Roger wrote I need more time
to pay your mortgage instalments
The $A has crumbled on hard currency markets
My purchasing parity theorem was wrong

Mr Wong's big black eyes counted to ten
and there was no answer
printed on the blue demy contracts under seal
secure in the Office of The White Oriolle
notarised copies under a dagger axe
that covered the map of New Greenville
and Wong Dynasty forecasts
made with Synthetic Option Technology

Shore Days

Five footers peak off the sound
The tubes are great
Low tide slides in
I'm alone to hit the stand-ups
hard as I like or pump out
to the dark side of a blaster
maroon myself
cilia singing in the inner ear
to bone-cave echoes
whale, shark voices, dynasties of fish

a sound no one else hears
the swell sucking the udder of the sea

I surf the morning glass a jade man
spinning the dollar of the sky
to get it on – rage in a time warp
locked in the ocean's gut
drunk till I die

I'm on a Double Flyer Swallow
a real thruster channeled front and back
that makes the bay move out
an' I'm stoked on a ledge
flying off the lip
tucked-in to crank a roller-coaster
right through the back door
then back to fire-dance the drop
power the tube, knees down
rail hard in the face
spaced out – I am the sea
breath a wind's triangle of the Tao
tracks carved in the wave

lines I willow across a slash session
stoked on airs and snaps and baz rolls
stroked onto the scroll of one day
until I'm surfed-out
and leave to carry home
the inside of a wave
the colour of the sky

Windows on the World

Molphy QC has chambers on the fiftieth level
of the IRC Building at Circular Quay
He watches every path the wind takes
every shadow cast by the sun
gestures of storms coming in from the Tasman
the perpetual present
swing from darkness to light
and back into darkness

At precisely 5AM he examines a brief
that outlines the history of Blue Dynamite
In front of him a view of the harbour
on a twenty thousand dollar day
a conference with Roger at 9AM
a mention before Mr. Justice Furore at 10
lunch at the Sydney Harbour Club
with a sinister friend
then a hand-up brief
containing terms of a settlement
not to be disclosed to anyone
followed by four conferences and an advice
on how to minimise an impending capital gain

The law of Mortgages sits quietly on the vellum desk
with Anson on Contracts still as a law student
An IBM work-station waits on-line
to a DEC twenty-sixty mainframe

He touches the keyboard as a gigolo
might touch the skin of his appointment book
feeds to IBM a menu of figures and facts
and all the *What if's* Roger has missed
and the *What then's* Ho Li Wong has not
sends them flying over the Pacific
through the Trade winds at Pipeline and Sunset
into a Knowledge Base of legal precedents
case and statute law, an inference system
linked by dialogue boxes in thirteen languages
to be vector processed through gigabytes of virtual memory
by CYBER and CRAY twenty-one

then reads the answer big macros
flashed to the display screen on the credenza

to be typed in snake-mode by the printer
quicker than any ordinary man
might say the name Dalrymple Nosegay

8AM being coffee time
he dingo slouched
past secretaries and floor managers
snarled at a barrister's clerk

Back at 9
to deal with Ho Li Wong versus Roger

Tracks

To go out beyond wave break
anywhere in the world
Angourie, Dakar, Honolua Bay
is to feel the sea's presence and pull
more than anything else
how close the sea comes
to hand's reflex
how a body is swallowed
by groundswells that ride in
from where storms spat
at mid-latitudes
measured big valleys on the run
and how all coastlines
wrapped in spools of silk
stitch sailmaker spaces
between surf and sun

Conference 9AM

That which is done is that which shall be done: and there
is no new thing under the sun

The QC listened to a story he hears
almost daily
from clients who enter his chambers
as suddenly as a Southerly Buster
blows along Macquarie Street
at the end of a summer's day

Roger pauses to ignore the view

Years of work down the tube
Got all Greenville
before the Third Airport was announced
Took options on Anderson's sheep station
to the west
RSL, old Mrs Parkes' grave, town monument

Law Reports tall as the ceiling
know where every day begins and ends
and do not move one buckram eyebrow
don't even blink

D9s have levelled Lytton Street
Wong and the Bank of Asia want the lot

The Law of Contracts
is silent as a newly admitted barrister

I've read the brief
It seemed like a good idea at the time
is the streaker's defence

The QC pointed to the display screen
ominous books reaching to the ceiling
glanced briefly through the window of the world
ferries passing Fort Denison, the Opera House

I fed you to the computer this morning
Checked the facts with data base
IBM's opinion is
you and Greenville are wiped out

He put on his wig and gown
shook hands gratuitiously

    I've got a matter in the Equity Court at 10

and left with a rustle of silk

Varuna in the Tube

You see everything in the face
of an old man and on the wall
of a wave step into the centre
of a mandala – colours pinwheeling
down steep alleys of the break
rail hard in and the fish listen

I push the limits
hand on a vertical
only room for one man
to measure force-lines
along this face
ride a reality
that only happens now

and the eye of the wave
is the eye of the hurricane
Glaciers are locked in it
forests of rain, ice caps
all the world's rivers
lakes, sacred springs
wells divined by seers, prophets
sinuous fluids of air
silts, flood wrack
plants that have died
and given back evaporates
the pterodactyls' thirst
convected skywards
or a gulf stream lost
when land masses
shunted over it

Worlds spin in the tunnel of a wave
infra-red light of all pre-dawns
The vessel of all that's possible

Rocks don't talk
The long front
edges past Endeavour Point
pearling and the spit stings
I touch the ocean
front the ridge
I'm home

I owned a big rhino
long and fast and clean
Some undersea shift sent her in
or a cyclone, a new island
isobars touching a storm circle
thousands of miles off
a fire-ring boiling the bottom of the world

The life of men and women pass like a galloping horse, changing at every turn, at every hour. What aught they do, or what aught they not do, except allow their own discomposition to continue.

– Chuan Tze.

Blue Dynamite